07/91
12.95

BASIC E

BASIC ®

SNOWSHOEING

Withdrawn from Collection

PHIL SAVIGNANO

The
Globe
Pequot
press

Guilford, Connecticut

Dedicated to my friend Mike Perry
for fostering my passion for the outdoors.

Copyright © 2001 by The Globe Pequot Press

All rights reserved. No part of this book may be reproduced or transmitted in any form by any means, electronic or mechanical, including photocopying and recording, or by any information storage and retrieval system, except as may be expressly permitted by the 1976 Copyright Act or by the publisher. Requests for permission should be made in writing to The Globe Pequot Press, P.O. Box 480, Guilford, Connecticut 06437.

Basic Essentials is a registered trademark of The Globe Pequot Press.

Cover design by Lana Mullen
Illustrations by M.A. Dubé
Text and layout design by Casey Shain
Cover photo courtesy Tubbs Snowshoes, Stowe, Vermont
Photo credits: pages vi,vii, 2, 5, and 6 courtesy Redfeather Snowshoes, Denver, Colorado; 7, 8, 9, 22, 29, 35, 36, 38, 40, 46, and 47 courtesy Tubbs Snowshoes, Stowe, Vermont.

Library of Congress Cataloging-in-Publication Data
Savignano, Phil
   Basic essentials. Snowshoeing/Phil Savignano.—1st ed.
     p. cm. — (Basic essentials series)
   ISBN 0-7627-0629-5
     1. Snowshoes and snowshoeing. I. Title: Snowshoeing. II. Title.
   GV853.S28 2000
   796.9'2—dc1   00-057809

Manufactured in the United States of America
First Edition/First Printing

Contents

Introduction

"If you can walk, you can cross-country ski" was the winter slogan of the 1980s. Well, that wasn't completely true; there really is a lot more to it than that. However, if you can walk, you can snowshoe, and the learning curve is so short you'll be wondering why you didn't do this sooner. The sport of snowshoeing is experiencing an incredible revival. No longer is it only transportation for the trapper, woodsman, or serious mountaineer. It is the perfect activity for the time-starved to easily get out for an hour and catch some fresh air and exercise and enjoy the magic of nature, tracking wildlife and soaking up the beauty of snow-filled woods. It is also a great alternative to dodging traffic while jogging slippery streets.

With the sudden growth in popularity has come a boom in equipment that is stronger and easier to use than the gear used by peoples migrating to North America thousands of years ago. High-tech fabrics and an understanding of "layering" clothing enable snowshoers to personalize their wardrobe for comfort in a wide range of weather and temperatures.

Snowshoeing is an inclusive sport. There is a place for anyone interested in enjoying fresh air and exercise to participate: old or young, fast or slow, for solitude or with friends, in the mountains or in the backyard. This book hopes to help the newcomer to snowshoeing start on the right foot; choose the right equipment, clothing, and accessories to be comfortable; learn enough technique so that the first excursion will be a success; and gain a sense of the demands of winter sports to enable the newcomer to make responsible decisions in the outdoors.

Figure 1 **Most contemporary snowshoers aren't aware of snowshoeing's ancient roots.**

Tracking the Past

For those curious about the history of snowshoeing, evidence indicates it originated in central Asia around 6,000 years ago. Solid, flat slabs of wood known as shoeskis were strapped to footwear that allowed ancient hunters to shuffle through the snow to forage or pursue game. As the population began migrating, the tribes that moved west into Europe and Scandinavia evolved these tools into skis. The tribes that migrated east developed the ancestors to the modern snowshoe. By the time people had traveled across the Bering Strait into North America snowshoe refinements allowed those early inhabitants to move freely in the deep snows of the north. As the Native Americans moved across the continent they adapted their snowshoes to meet the varying demands of the snow conditions in the area where they settled. In areas where the snow was light and dry, they designed shoes with large surface area and finely woven decking to provide maximum flotation. In the other areas where the snow was dense, wet or icy, narrower snowshoes with a more open weave evolved. They chose frame materials that were strong, light, and could be manipulated into the shapes they needed. The decking was made of woven reeds or rawhide, frames were fashioned of ash.

It wasn't until the early 1800s—when Scandinavians began immigrating to the Americas—that skis were introduced to the New World. Prior to that time snowshoes ruled the North Country as the means of snow travel. As Europeans started exploring the continent, access to the deep wilderness was restricted to waterways during the warmer seasons. When snow filled the woods, travel would have ceased without the snowshoe. Trade furthered the growth of snowshoeing with an ever-growing market for furs. Trappers worked hard through the winter, keeping their lines open, maintaining traps, and building their inventory for spring, when ice out on waterways would mark the opening of commercial trade routes. High demand encouraged the trappers to expand the territory, develop stronger relations with the native peoples, and always push farther into the New World looking for more lucrative trapping grounds.

Snowshoeing was strictly a transportation tool until the 1700s, when it started to evolve as a sport. At first it was used as a competitive military drill to develop preparedness of troops on winter maneuvers. By the 1800s its popularity had grown in Canada, and clubs began to emerge. Drawing on the military heritage, teams would wear bright uniforms, stage parades, and compete in a variety of activities. In

Figure 2 **Snowshoe club events are a great way to enjoy the outdoors and make new friends at the same time.**

Quebec there were so many club teams that in 1907 they formed the Canadian Snowshoer's Union. The interest soon spread to the United States, and clubs began to form, as did the spirit of international competition. To this day, especially in areas with a strong Franco-American heritage, many of these clubs still exist and continue to hold events with all the pageantry of the past.

Like skis, their distant relative, snowshoes have gone to both the North Pole and South Pole and helped with exploration of the snowy, remote regions of the world. They have gone to war and moved troops in areas where no other tool or vehicle could be relied upon. They've supported climbing expeditions in some of the tallest mountains in the world.

Even with the rebirth of snowshoeing's popularity the basic principle of design have not changed in centuries. Certainly there have been many advances in material to make snowshoes lighter, stronger, and easier to maintain, but when you put on a pair of snowshoes and go, you'll be experiencing the same freedom of winter travel as those persons did thousands of years before.

BASIC ESSENTIALS

Selecting a Snowshoe

If variety is the spice of life, then the choice of snowshoes is well seasoned. When you go to a shop, you're going to find a wall of snowshoes in all sizes and shapes. You're probably thinking "I just wanted to go for a walk in the woods; what did I get myself into?" Well, you're on the right track if you have a mental image of what you want to do on your snowshoes. Three quick questions will make selection very simple: What do you want to do most of the time? How much do you weigh? How much do you want to spend? The answers to these questions will narrow your choices to just a few pairs of shoes and a decision on aesthetics.

If you truly want to have an enjoyable experience snowshoeing, the selection process should not be based on what you found in your parents' or grandparents' attic. Just imagine hiking in someone else's boots or jogging in someone else's sneakers. It's the same thing, unless you're the same size and you're using them exactly as they did. As a kid I would borrow my Dad's snowshoes to pack cross-country ski trails. I spent a lot of time recovering from face plants in the snow. I'd either step on a shoe I was trying to lift or I'd catch the tip in unbroken snow. I resorted to taking wide, exaggerated steps, looking more like someone just back from the last cattle drive to Dodge than someone having fun in the snow. Criteria for selecting snowshoes include:

What do you want to do most of the time?

This is the most important question to ask yourself. It is very important to be honest with the answer so that your snowshoes will match

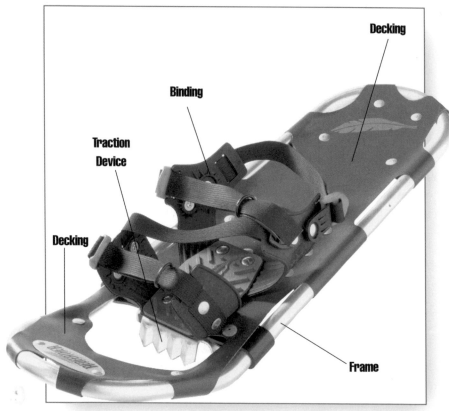

Decking

Binding

Traction
Device

Decking

Frame

Figure 3   **Anatomy of a snowshoe.**

the type of real activity you choose to do most often. Knowing your
personal end use will help you pick out a style that functions favorably
nearly every time you go snowshoeing. It will make the difference
between eagerly grabbing your gear to head out and making excuses
for putting it off to another day.

Consider these activity choices:

◆ Do you see yourself hiking in the mountains with a full
summit pack on your back, teched out with an ice ax, plastic
hiking boots, and a GPS navigating device?

◆ Or are you carrying a full backpack, dragging a sled into a
remote, backcountry location for a winter camping
experience?

♦ If you are purely a recreational snowshoeist, you may have visions of hiking with friends and family on old Jeep trails or around the back nine at the local golf course, stopping for lunch at a scenic, snow-covered spot out of the wind.

♦ Do part of your winter-workout plans include dashing out at lunch for a quick forty-minute run in the park or going out first thing in the morning with your dog?

Whatever your expectation may be, there is a snowshoe designed to make that experience as easy as possible. What may be great for one activity, however, may not do so well for another. To choose a snowshoe that matches your needs, look at the requirements of your vision and pair them up with the features of different snowshoes.

How much do you weigh?

Your personal weight, in conjunction with your expectations of the equipment, must be considered in choosing the right snowshoes for you.

Features to consider

Flotation: First and foremost, you want flotation. Flotation doesn't mean you'll hover above the snow or walk clean on top of the snow; it does mean that it will support your weight and prevent you from sinking in up to your hip. The amount of sinkage depends upon the type of snow you're walking on. Light powder offers the least resistance, so you will probably leave a deep impression. Spring corn snow is fairly dense, so with the right snowshoe you may sink in only a couple of inches. With your weight distributed over a firm crust, you may only leave scratch marks on the surface. Your goal is to float as high as possible while maintaining a comfortable amount of maneuverability. The greater the surface area of a snowshoe, the higher you will float. A general rule of thumb is one square inch per pound being carried (that includes your weight). Solid-decking snowshoes have more flotation than laced decks. If you are trail breaking into the backcountry where the snow lays undisturbed, carrying a significant amount of weight on your back, you'll need maximum flotation. If you are running to keep in shape, most likely you are using packed trails either at a cross-country ski center, snowmobile trails, or a regularly traveled trail, and your flotation needs will be minimal. For a recreational snowshoeist your needs fall somewhere between the two, spending most of your time on established trails but sometimes breaking your own. The biggest snowshoes will be cumbersome, the running shoes won't provide enough flotation for exploring. Choose a snowshoe that is designed for your weight; if you are on the border-line, opt for the smaller snowshoe.

Maneuverability: Another feature to look for is maneuverability. If you are hiking in the woods or the mountains, you'll need a snowshoe that can easily be maneuvered. In underbrush or tight trails, you'll want snowshoes that can be turned easily without tangling. Out in open country it is more desirable to have snowshoes that track.

Size: The most obvious factor in maneuverability is size. Both width and length will have an effect. Snowshoes designed for high flotation will certainly be more awkward than small shoes. Here's an advantage to having solid-deck snowshoes: They don't need to be as wide as laced-deck shoes, so they will be smaller. You will still need to set a priority for yourself if you are looking at backcountry/mountaineering snowshoes. Recreational snowshoes should have superior agility, and, of course, if you are running on your snowshoes, the smaller the better.

Other things that affect maneuverability are the balance and the bindings:

Balance: A snowshoe's balance is important to your ease of walking and climbing. Ideally the tail is a little heavier than the toe so that, with each step, the toe of the shoe will rise to prevent tripping. A little weight in the tail is a good thing. Tails aid in steering as you make step turns. It is easier to turn your foot if the back of the snowshoe offers a little resistance. Weight in the tails also provides tracking to the snow-shoe. This is an energy saver over the long haul. Too much weight in the back will cause excess drag and create extra work.

Bindings: Aside from size, the biggest single factor contributing to maneuverability are the bindings. Bindings hold the snowshoes to your feet. Having a feel for the snow depends upon great control of the snowshoe. Bindings need to give torsional responsiveness to your feet, allowing you to steer and kick steps into the snow. The best way to achieve this is with rotating binding, a mounting plate that attaches to a solid bar under the ball of the foot. This is how the best moun-taineering and backcountry snowshoes are set up. Because of the hardware, it adds a little extra weight and expense.

Some recreational and running snowshoes use pivot bindings and generally cost less. Rivets or screws attach to the decking. This works fine on packed trails, but the flex softens the control in deep snow and on icy conditions.

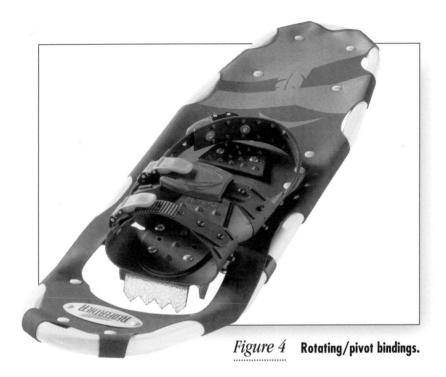

Figure 4   **Rotating/pivot bindings.**

There are many different bindings to choose from. Some things to keep in mind when you're selecting a binding are ease of entry, ease of adjustment, ability to hold adjustments after use, and fit to your footwear.

Traditional bindings like the H or K styles, which look great with wooden snowshoes, are made of leather. Leather gets wet from melting snow and stretches, causing frequent adjustments on the trail. Getting wet or even soggy means icing, and that can make for a very frustrating experience, especially when attempting to make adjustments on frozen gear with gloves or mittens.

Traditional bindings made with synthetic materials hold their fit better but are complicated to mount and adjust. There are many pieces to tweak to get a perfect fit, and if you are sharing snowshoes with a friend, it gets pretty involved. Most new bindings are made with non-stretching synthetics. These have a toe-stop built in and quickly adjust with cams or buckles.

Bindings also need to allow you to walk naturally, allowing your foot to step freely through the toe hole for traction.

Traction devices: Snow conditions and terrain dictate the need for traction. Soft snow on gradual terrain and most any snowshoe

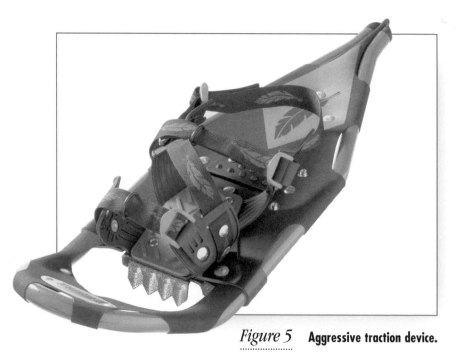

Figure 5   **Aggressive traction device.**

frame will give you enough traction to move. But packed, crusty, and icy conditions will challenge even the most experienced snowshoeist. Toe and heel crampons provide essential climbing and descending grip. These are spikes, usually aluminum, under the toe and heel. Some snowshoes have aggressive crampons on the toe of the bindings to afford exceptional grip for climbing. Mountaineering shoes have this type, as well as very important heel crampons which add control on descents. Running/fitness snowshoes will also have toe and heel crampons to give traction for acceleration and control. One-piece molded shoes have traction teeth built into the snowshoe, but better models add metal teeth or studs along with crampons for the iciest conditions. Traction devices can be added to most snowshoes and are sold separately.

These factors will put you in the right section of the snowshoe department and help you narrow your choices to more specific needs. There are other details to be considered, however, before you strap your snowshoes onto your feet and head off on the trail.

With the explosion of snowshoe popularity over the past few years, the issue of walking on snow has received a myriad of technological solutions. In fact, when you go to the snowshoe shop, you'll find the traditional laced snowshoes are given less attention than ever. Now when you walk past the racks, you will see all sorts of shapes, colors, materials, and prices.

How much do you want to spend?

What you really want to know now is what you are getting for the money.

Snowshoe frames

Wooden frames: Traditional wooden snowshoes are aesthetically pleasing. They have carried people over the snow for thousands of years. The bent-ash frames come in the widest variety of shapes and sizes, reflecting the historical needs of the people who designed them and the environments in which they lived. Traditionally strung with rawhide and shellacked for protection from moisture and wear, they have a natural beauty and appeal for those who appreciate hand-crafted workmanship. The wooden frames and rawhide lacing require routine maintenance. Many wooden frames are also available with neoprene lacing, which saves some of the maintenance. Neoprene isn't as stiff as well-shellacked rawhide, so you should expect a little bouncier ride. Well-cared-for wooden framed shoes are very tough; however, they are the weakest of all the frame materials and so caution must be used in

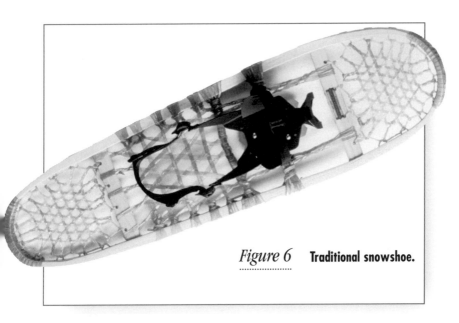

Figure 6   **Traditional snowshoe.**

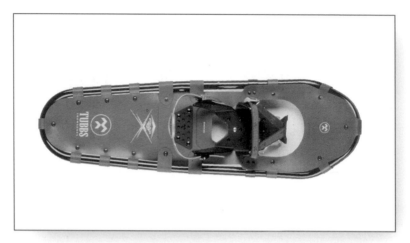

Figure 7 **Aluminum-frame snowshoe.**

difficult terrain to avoid bridging fractures (see Chapter 7) or broken laces.

Aluminum frames: The introduction of aircraft aluminum tubing as a frame material radically changed the look of snowshoes. More expensive than wood, they are lighter, and considerably stronger. Certainly valued features for the mountaineer, these also make them highly appealing for recreational snowshoeing and racing. Nearly maintenance free, more expensive shoes have an anodized coating to prevent corrosion.

Nearly all aluminum snowshoes have solid decks rather than laced decks. The solid decks provide greater flotation per square inch, the advantage being comparable flotation in smaller, less awkward, more maneuverable snowshoes. Decks are made of a variety of materials and combinations of materials: rugged neoprene, quiet Hypalon, and lightweight plastics. All have smooth surfaces that spill snow easily with each step.

Molded frames: One-piece snowshoes are the most recent innovation in frame construction. Molded of durable plastics, they're inexpensive in comparison with the other types. Excellent recreational snowshoes that offer a stable platform are MSR snowshoes, which have an attachable piece for increased flotation, and Lexan snowshoes, which have proven to be stronger and more resilient than aluminum shoes. Traction is designed into the molds, but many also have attached crampons or studs for added grip.

Figure 8 **Molded-frame snowshoe.**

Composite-material frames: Space-age materials have also found
a home in the snow. Making extremely lightweight and strong snowshoes, mostly for the racer, carbon fiber has been used for tubing and
even solid-deck snowshoes. Generally speaking, these are quite pricey
in comparison with other shoes, but if you are looking to shave
ounces off your feet without sacrificing durability, they are worth the
money.

Snowshoes for Kids

Kids love to go snowshoeing. The freedom, the surreal surround-
ings, and the intriguing little tracks capture their attention (see
Chapter 6: Snowshoeing with Kids).

With the recent surge in the sport's popularity, there is a great
selection of affordable snows for kids. Equipment choices are very sim-
ilar to adult gear: wood, aluminum, and molded. The molded snowshoes are available in a wide selection of fun colors; some even have
animal tracks molded into the footprint.

Snowshoe selection is based on a child's weight. For younger kids,
think smaller and lighter as better. Not only do children have shorter
steps, but they also have a narrower stance. Smaller snowshoes will
be less awkward, and after all, kids won't be breaking many trails. The
biggest challenge is with bindings. Growing kids are hard to keep up
with; sometimes they seem to grow a piece at a time, legs one day and
a foot the next. Oftentimes they'll be all kid except their feet. Take

their boots in while picking out snowshoes to be sure the bindings are big enough. The least expensive snowshoes will have permanently attached bindings; more expensive ones can be removed and exchanged for a more suitable piece.

Remember, the most important factor in choosing a snowshoe is to select one you will use often and have fun on. Try a bunch out before you make a purchase. There are demo days and rental centers wherever there is snow.

Technique

First Steps

One of the great aspects of snowshoeing is that the learning curve is so short. It doesn't take long to get comfortable with the equipment. There aren't many technical parts to the technique, so, within hours, you'll be able to get to the real lure of snowshoeing, enjoying the outdoors and fresh air.

If you've never snowshoed before, spend a little time in an area that is packed out. This will give you time to get familiar with the feel of snowshoes on your feet, to see how the tails drop as you lift your foot, and to see how much you'll need to lift your foot so that the snowshoe is clear of the snow. The rest of snowshoeing technique will come from

Figure 9
....

This stable and well-balanced stance places the snowshoeist in a good position to begin most maneuvers.

Figure 10

Side-stepping. Here, the snowshoeist moves sideways in an uphill direction. Each foot is placed firmly before the other foot is lifted.

experience as you walk in different snow conditions, from deep, fresh snow to hard-packed crust. The following are the basics that will make your experience easier.

Side-stepping:

Side-stepping is a maneuvering skill, and it is exactly what it sounds like, stepping laterally. This may not seem like a big deal until you try it with snowshoes in deep snow. If you hurry, it is easy to step on your shoes, get caught in the deep snow, and end up packing a trail with

your face. When you get the technique down, you can move pretty quickly.

Weight the foot opposite the direction you want to step. Once your footing is solid, lift the unweighted foot straight up until the whole snowshoe leaves the snow. Now step out to the side the width of a snowshoe. When your footing is solid, weight that foot and bring the other shoe over. The key is to commit all your weight to one foot before lifting the other, making sure the stepping foot is clear of any entanglements.

Snowshoeing

Figure 11

The step-turn. The snowshoeist turns ninety degrees, ending in a stable and well-balanced stance.

Step turns are a variation of sidestepping. The subtle difference is that it is the forepart of your snowshoe that makes the step. Again, a little at a time. Easy enough in packed snow, but practice in deep snow.

Walking is walking—left right, left right. The only real difference to your normal stride is the need to consciously pick up your feet. It's a lot like walking in ankle-deep water. No problem when you're fresh, but as the miles go by and you start to fatigue, it's natural to shuffle

and easy to get tripped up. In unpacked snow pace yourself and take frequent breaks. If you're breaking trails with a group, everyone should take a turn in front. Don't be a hero; take twenty steps and let the group go by so that you can walk in the packed-out trail.

Reversing direction without stepping on your shoes is trickier than it sounds, especially with long snowshoes. If there is plenty of space, the easiest way to turn 180 degrees is with a simple step turn. In tighter quarters you may need to use a kick turn.

Snowshoeing   **15**

Figure 12

The kick-turn. The snowshoeist turns completely around, ending in a stable stance. The key is bringing your leading foot up and turning it 180 degrees, then following with your other foot.

Kick turns are for reversing direction in a limited amount of space. Before starting make sure you have solid footing with both feet. To initiate the turn, kick the toe of your snowshoe high enough to use the heel as a pivot point. Once your snowshoe has cleared the snow, rotate your foot and hips 180 degrees and plant it in the track

you've already made behind you. Shift your weight to this foot, kick the other foot clear of the snow, and step around to face the other direction. This can be an unstable maneuver the first couple of times it is tried, but using ski poles for balance will make it more comfortable (see Figure 12).

Figure 13

Getting up from a fall. Roll onto your back to get your ski poles out of the snow, then roll back over, crossing your poles in the snow in front of you for support. *Now* stand up, pushing against the crossed ski poles with your arms.

Getting up after falling down: Yes, sooner or later you'll end up in the snow as a tangled blob. Aside from a little damage to your pride, the worst that is going to happen is that some snow will get down your neck. But you may find getting back on your feet a challenge if the snow is deep. Don't try to leap to your feet in an attempt to avoid notice; you'll be covered with snow anyway, so everyone will know exactly what happened. First thing, untangle— take your hands out of the ski-pole straps, but *hang onto your poles.* Roll onto your back and get your feet in the air. Then roll onto your stomach and get on your hands and knees. Make an x with your poles on the snow for support (don't try to push yourself up with the poles jabbed into the snow; it puts a lot of stress on your shoulders). From the kneeling position, sit up on your heels, and put one foot up; now with your poles gripped by the shaft for balance, stand up (see Figure 13).

Climbing

The shortest distance between two points may be a straight line, but when you're climbing in deep snow, it's usually the steepest and the most strenuous. Climbing is certainly easier with the new snowshoes that have cleats built into the bindings, but there are a couple of techniques that will make the ascent less work. A gradual climb won't feel much different from walking, but as the grade steepens, you will start to lose traction if you don't make some adjustments to your technique.

Going up: Think of going up a ladder and concentrate on stepping with your toes and not the snowshoes. Because the snowshoes pivot at the ball of your foot, they will try to stay on top of the snow and follow the contour of the slope. You need to step with your toes as though you were stepping on the rungs of a ladder. Your traction and balance are better if you maintain a vertical position and don't lean into the hill. (If you are using poles, remember to let your legs do the work and avoid trying to pull yourself up hill.)

Kick steps are important when the going gets steep. It's the same principle as climbing the ladder except you will need to kick into the hill and punch your steps. Especially in soft snow make sure your footing is solid before taking the next step. Taking long strides is really taxing, so save your energy and take small steps, which will allow you to rest between moves.

Traversing is an easier way to climb because it allows you to control the grade. Save your energy and enjoy the views on the way up. In soft snow try to keep your feet as level as possible by kicking the side of your snowshoe into the snow. Your goal is to create a solid platform that enables you to take your next step. Your tempo becomes step-half step-step-half step. Side stepping allows you to rest on any given step.

Descending

Once you've found the easy way up, you'll need a few tools to get back down. Going down can be an adventure by itself. Not so much on a gradual incline, but as the trail gets steeper and your weight ends up on the tails of your snowshoes, you will lose traction.

Flexed knees are the key to keeping the snowshoes' cleats engaged and maintaining traction. Small steps are more secure than big steps. Like climbing, the best way to control the steepness of the climb is by traversing down.

Glissading is a more advanced and fun way to get down once you've gained confidence in control and comfort with your equipment. Using your ski poles as a rudder, take your hands out of the straps and hold both grips in one hand. With the other hand grasp the poles about 6 inches above the baskets. Squat down and reach back with the baskets. Your weight should be on the backs of the snowshoes, and you will start to slide. Control your speed by weighting and unweighting the ski poles. Keeping the poles tight to your hip will enable you to add an element of steering to your glide. Practice this on a small hill before trying it out on the trail.

There is not a lot to getting comfortable on snowshoes—an afternoon with friends at the local park or golf course and you'll be ready for the trail. Experience is going to be your best instructor; however, common sense and good judgment will allow you to gain experience. If you are just starting out, keep it fun. Go where you know the terrain and always turn back while you're still having fun.

Dressing for Winter

othing will ruin a winter outing faster than being too cold or, believe it or not, too hot. Snowshoeing is an active sport. No matter how fast you travel over the snow, you burn calories, and that generates heat. The trick to staying comfortable in the outdoors is in how you manage that heat. Just the right amount lets your body maintain a core body temperature of 98.6 degrees F and function normally. If the temperature drops below that, you will start to feel the effect of hypothermia. It doesn't have to be below freezing for that to occur; it can happen anytime when temperatures are below 55 degrees F and especially when wetness is involved.

Your first defense against these conditions is how you dress. Here's the challenge—stay warm, not hot; dress so that you can regulate your temperature, adjusting for the weather and your work level; and stay dry. *The best way to do this is to dress in comfortable layers.* Learn to dress in layers to create a personal climate that allows you to regulate your temperature. You'll be surprised at how much control you actually have.

There are three major thieves of heat: conduction, convection, and evaporation. The right selection of clothing will eliminate their effects on you and even let you use them to your advantage.

Conduction is the transfer of heat into another object. Consider your body is trying to heat the environment around you and vice versa. If you were to sit in a snow bank without insulation, your body would try to heat the snow up to 98.6 degrees F at the same time the snow would be trying to chill your body to a subfreezing temperature. Which do you think would win? Sitting in a snowbank sounds silly, but

Figure 14   **Layering of modern water-resistant and breathable fabrics makes snowshoe travel safe and comfortable in all but the most severe winter conditions.**

think about ears trying to heat an earring all day or your feet trying to heat wet socks all day.

Convection is the transfer of heat into the air. Imagine how hard your furnace would work if you left the windows wide open all the time. Imagine the fuel cost. The same thing is happening to you if you are not protected. The circulating air is constantly robbing your heat.

Evaporation is a close friend of convection. With evaporation there is cooling by moisture vaporizing. Wet clothing exposed to air, if it doesn't freeze first, will evaporate and lower your body temperature. A sweating head is like a chimney with an open flue with heat pouring out the top.

Layering

Layering allows you to create a personal climate control. A layering system of clothing allows you to customize your personal environment based on weather conditions and your metabolism. It's important to stay dry, warm, and protected from weather. Think of three Ws: Wicking, Warmth, and Weather, which correspond to the three major functions a layering system should provide.

Wicking: moisture movement, keeping your skin dry so that you are not using your energy to heat wet clothing

Warmth: insulation that traps your heat in comfortable quantities, without getting too warm

Weather: protection against rain, snow, and wind

First Layer

Start closest to your skin with *long underwear;* staying dry is crucial at this layer. You're going to perspire, especially if you are working hard, so it's important to *wick* that moisture out and away from direct contact with your skin.

Most good synthetics are breathable and nonabsorbent. They are designed to let vapor pass through the fabric to the outside, where it can evaporate away from the skin or transfer it to the next layer of clothing. Power Dry, Capilene, CoolMax, and polypropylene are lightweight materials compared with traditional natural fibers.

Quality long underwear usually comes in a choice of fabric weights: light, medium, and expedition. This allows you to custom dress for the cold and amount of exposure you'll be facing. For instance, with temperatures in the 20s, if I'm out for a workout, lightweight may be all that I need because I won't be hanging around outdoors when I'm done, whereas, on a day hike, with stops and longer exposure to the cold, the medium weight may be more appropriate. If I'm out for a slow walk, however, looking for wildlife and taking pictures, I'll dress in expedition weight because I won't be generating a lot of heat. The heavier the fabric, the warmer the underwear, as it will also serve as insulation. Most of the synthetics are machine washable and dryable so they can be used day after day. Wool is a more traditional fabric and is an O.K. insulator; however, it does hold some moisture and, depending on the quality, can be a little scratchy. Don't use cotton long underwear; it gets wet and stays wet. You don't want that in the winter. *Tip:* Long underwear should be form fitting to work best.

Second Layer

Insulation is the key to *warmth.* This layer doesn't create heat, it traps the heat you generate. This isn't necessarily a single piece of clothing, either; you can wear many layers of insulation. The goal here is to maintain a normal body temperature while enjoying a winter environment. If you are normally cold, you'll probably require a little more insulation. If you get hot easily, plan on it and dress lighter.

Your insulation layer should offer you a lot of flexibility. It can start with a light layer of a polyester fleece or a wool shirt (remember, you don't want to be wet) that can be covered by an insulated jacket of down or a nonabsorbent synthetic. If you are going for a day trip and plan on making stops, you won't want to wear a heavy layer of insulation because you will quickly get hot, so pack along a vest or jacket or even some insulated pants for longer stops. *Goose down* is great. It's very light and can pack down small enough to fit a day pack or fanny pack. The biggest liability of down is moisture from inside as well as out. Good down is a very fluffy cluster that comes from very fine goose feathers. Its high loft creates a natural dead-air space to trap heat, but when it gets wet, it just won't work. So, this is not a good choice for rainy or really wet snow conditions. Many great synthetic insulators like Polarguard, Quallofill, Thinsulate, and Primaloft don't absorb moisture. They work similarly to down by trapping heat in their fibers. Thinsulate does this without the bulky loft, while Primaloft is also remarkably compressible.

24

Third Layer

The last and outermost layer is to protect you from the *weather*. This layer should give you wind and water protection. A simple nylon shell is one of the most versatile garments you can own. It usually packs well and can be worn over your long underwear or over an insulating layer. If it has a hood, all the better to protect the back of your neck, cover your ears, and prevent heat loss through the top of your head. A shell is usually water resistant, which means it will keep you dry in a light, dry snow or light mist. In prolonged exposure, however, it will eventually soak through. It could be water-repellent, meaning it will shed light rain or wet snow for awhile. To be truly waterproof, it needs to withstand driving rain and have all exposed seams sealed against leaking.

Because you are snowshoeing and generating heat and moisture from within, *breathability* is a factor that needs serious consideration. Certainly the best fabric would be one that is both breathable and waterproof. There are a number of products out there that fill this niche. Gore-Tex is the leader, but you'll also find others like Entrant and H2Off. If you're looking for something to wear for a workout, then you may want to lean toward something more breathable and less waterproof. A couple of high-performance fabrics do this really nicely: Both Activent from Gore and EPIC by Nextec are extremely lightweight and packable as well as highly water repellent.

With outer layers you will find ventilation is a good thing if you have control of it. Look for shells that have deep front zippers. A zipper can be like a thermostat: When your temperature rises, lower the zipper; when you get cold, raise the zipper. Another great feature to have are pit-zips for under your arms. These are great for blowing days when you don't want to leave your front exposed but you are still generating lots of heat. Look for zipper pulls you can adjust with mittens or gloves on.

All these layers work together in different combinations and need to be adjustable enough for you to accommodate changes in both the weather and your activity level. It may take a little while to figure out a system that meets your needs, but once you do, you'll be able to stay comfortable in pretty much any kind of weather. The key is to select clothing that allows you to be flexible.

Layering Your Head, Hands, and Feet

Don't forget to layer your hands, head, and feet. The same principles apply. Your number-one thermostat control is your head. You lose as much as 80 percent of your heat through your head. The best hat is one that lets you regulate your heat loss. Look for one that can be pulled down over your ears and cover the back of your neck when you're cold. As you warm up, it can sit on the top of your head. If you are working hard, like hill climbing, take it off and tuck it in an easily accessed pocket.

Hands and feet need a light, wicking layer to keep them dry. You'll find gloves, mittens, and socks in the same materials as long underwear, materials that will increase your comfort without bulk. Mittens are warmer than gloves because your fingers can share the heat. If you prefer the dexterity of gloves but get cold, one solution is a hybrid that looks like a lobster claw. *Never* wear cotton on your feet in winter! The last thing you want is wet feet. Think how much heat it will take to keep wet socks from freezing. It's also important to remember that more socks won't necessarily make warmer feet. Too many socks will ruin the fit of your boots and can actually restrict the circulation in your feet. Find the balance.

Choosing the Right Footwear

You can dress your body in layers but what do you do with your feet? Choosing the right footwear is a lot like selecting the right type of snowshoe. Footwear should match the type of snowshoeing you are planning. Are you going backpacking, day hiking, or out for a workout? Unless your activity will involve a great deal of standing around, warmth is not the most important feature you are searching for, it is on the list, but probably behind stability, dryness, and weight.

Stability: Because snowshoes are so much wider than your feet and because the snow doesn't give solid footing it is most important that your footwear gives you enough support to edge and turn your snowshoes. If you are mountaineering or backpacking, plastic boots or double leather boots will give you rigid soles needed to kick steps and for hard edging on traverses. The extra weight added is justified by the gain in control. If you are out for walks or day trips the same light hiking boots you use during the rest of the year should provide adequate support and control.

Dryness: Here your primary concern should be whether or not they will keep your feet dry. Wet feet are in danger of frostbite when they get cold and also steal heat from the rest of your body to keep moisture from getting cold. Two considerations are if your feet are getting wet from the outside in or the inside out. From the outside means that your boots aren't waterproof or snow is coming in from the top. All leather or Gore-Tex boots are best. Leather boots need to be kept waterproof by applying a sealant like SnowSeal or Nik Wax. Gore-Tex is a waterproof laminent that also breathes and lets moisture vapor inside your boots escape. Gaiters make a big difference if you are in deep snow. The gaiter covers the laces and the top of the boot to the top of your calf. They strap under the top of the boot to the top of your calf. They strap under the arch to hold them in position. These are available in a variety of coated nylons. If you are planning on a lot of bushwhacking, get ones made of a rugged Cordura or ballistic nylon; both are highly abrasion resistant. Gaiters are also available in Gore-Tex, which are worth every penny in comfort because they allow heat and vapor to vent from the top of your boots.

Weight: Heavy boots are just that, heavy. The snowshoes add enough weight so go light. Fitness snowshoeing is usually done on a packed trail so torsional stability is not a priority for the runner. Going light and keeping dry are first on the list when you are looking for speed. Run in sneakers with a short gaiter. It is important to find a sneaker that will keep your feet dry and there are a number of high-top winter running shoes or snow sneakers available. If you are day hiking, the same lightweight or medium-weight hiking boots you use in the summer and fall should be adequate.

Remember that you are creating a custom-clothing system for yourself. Don't be afraid to experiment. It's awfully easy to look at the outside temperature from a warm house and feel the cold. The tendency is to overdress for winter activities. Start a little cold and add layers, as you need them. If you are with a group, plan an early stop to adjust layers. Toughing it out doesn't help anyone, and you'll be surprised how many others are dying to add or subtract a layer.

Fitness Factor

J ogging in winter is messy at the least and dangerous at worst. Sidewalks are treacherous; streets are slippery, slushy, and narrower than usual; soft shoulders are buried; and footing is uncertain in the roads.

On the other hand, where there is snow there is the potential for a great workout that keeps you out of traffic and doesn't pound your knees. Depending on snow conditions, walking or running an hour on snowshoes will easily burn up to a thousand calories. Ski poles aren't just for balance; you can increase the aerobic value of your workout another 15 percent by using ski poles and gaining an upper-body workout with your time. Snowshoeing is good for your whole cardio-vascular system.

Places for Workout

Don't let travel be a deterrent to getting in a short workout. During winter there are many areas that are nearly forgotten about that may be close to home or work. Local athletic or recreational facilities like soccer fields, tracks, or Little League fields are usually minutes away. There may not be a lot of variety in terrain or very scenic, but once you've packed a trail, they are great places to get out to catch some fresh air. Local parks will offer a little more interesting terrain, and once covered with snow, you can design your own trail network. Golf courses offer a great variety of hills and flats, and even a nine-hole course should give you a big loop. Stay away from the greens, and most operations won't object to being used. Put on a headlamp and you can beat the winter gloom.

Figure 15 **Running in snowshoes.**

Stretching Exercises

When you make time for your workout, plan time to stretch. Stretching is one of the easiest ways to prevent injury, improve circulation, and increase range of motion. It is also one of the easiest parts of a workout to skimp on or, even worse, skip altogether. For a stretch to be effective, muscles need to fatigue, then relax. Usually, that means holding a stretch for at least twenty seconds for the benefit to begin. If a stretch causes pain, back off to a point of resistance. Avoid bouncing during stretches; this makes you vulner-

Snowshoeing   **29**

able to injury and doesn't let the muscle fatigue. Repeat each of the stretches three times. It is best not to stretch cold muscles even if you are indoors for your routine. Take them after a light warm up of five to ten minutes before you start.

Break your stretching into two categories: indoor stretches and trail stretches.

Indoor Stretches

Indoor stretches can be done at home in the morning while the coffee is brewing. These are lying-down stretches that, if done every day, will improve flexibility. Only the hardiest of souls would want to do these in the snow. Here's a quick routine:

Elongation: Lie down on your back, point your toes away, and reach your hands over your head. Keep your back flat and your shoulders square. Relax and point your toes toward your head and push your heels away.

Low Back Press: With bent knees, press the small of your back into the floor. Keep your shoulders and hips flat and your eyes on the ceiling.

Hamstring and Hip Flexor Stretch: From the same position as the Low Back Press, clasp one leg by the shin and pull your knee to your chest. At the same time straighten the other leg until it is parallel to the floor. Repeat the other side.

Straight Quad Stretch: Don't change positions yet. Point your left leg to the ceiling and grasp it with both hands high on the calf. Now straighten your right leg until it is flat on the floor. Repeat the other side.

Double Knee Pull: Still in the same position, draw both knees to your chest and try to touch your forehead to your knees.

Wishbone Stretch: From a sitting position spread your feet wide until you have constant resistance. Lean to the middle (you should feel this in the small of your back and not in your shoulders). Next face your right foot and, pressing your chest toward your thigh, reach with both hands to the soles of your feet. Keep your chin up. Repeat the other side.

Sole Press: From the wishbone bring the soles of your feet together.

Keeping your knees as low as possible, slowly pull your feet in as close as you can.

Time to change position. Lie on your stomach for the next part of the routine:

Full stretch: Same as the elongation stretch. For variety lift your arms and legs off the floor so that you are making contact only with your stomach.

The Swim: From the Full Stretch position, raise your right arm and left leg off the floor and hold. Then repeat your left arm and right leg in a slow rhythmic exchange for fifteen counts on each side.

Now get up on your hands and knees for the finale:
Cat Stretch: Reach forward with open palms on the floor. Roll your shoulders and arch your back. Next press your hips to the floor and raise your chin.

Trail Stretches

When you arrive at a trailhead, mentally you are ready to get going. After all, you've probably been cooped up in a car looking forward to strapping on your gear. The last thing you want to do is stop and stretch for ten minutes. But ten minutes now will probably save you a day's worth of sore muscles or worse. You can still get your gear right on and start out on the trail. You should never stretch while you're cold, anyway, so hike until you're warm, look for a protected space out of the wind, and loosen up. Use the natural setting to make it more interesting. Try to be as muscle specific as possible, stretching your lower back, hamstrings, quadriceps, calves, and shoulders.

Virtual Hula-Hoop: For hips and lower back, start by slowly making small circles with your hips and steadily increasing the size of the rotation. Keep your shoulders as stationary as possible. One way to do this is by planting your poles with outstretched arms. Rotate in both directions.

Pole-Toe Touch: For low back and hamstrings, hold your poles together with both hands. With arms stretched high over your head and knees slightly flexed, bend forward to touch your snowshoes. When you return to the upright position reach high and back.

Telemark/Lunge: Step forward into a lunge position with your weight evenly distributed between both feet. Your forward leg should be slightly flexed. Keeping your heel flat on the snowshoe of your trailing leg, flex forward for hamstrings and calves. Switch sides.

The Gracious Bow: From the same lunge position, move your hips back, flex your trailing leg, and bow at the waist. You will feel the stretch in the forward-leg hamstring.

Quad Stretch: With feet at shoulder width, lift your right foot to your buttocks. Stabilize yourself with a ski pole. Repeat on the other side.

Torso Twist: Rest your ski poles across your shoulders and hang your arms over the poles. With your feet at shoulder width and knees slightly flexed, twist as far as you can to the right. Return to center and do the same to the left. Return to center and try to touch your right elbow to your side and then to the left.

Reminders

Remember to stretch until there is resistance and not if there is pain. Hold each stretch for at least twenty seconds. Repeat each stretch three times. Don't bounce. If you want to feel really good after a trek, repeat the stretch routines at the end of your workout.

Even the best workouts can get boring. Try to mix up your routine by adding variety. One of the easiest ways to avoid the boredom of running the same route day after day is to change directions once in awhile and run it in reverse. If you are using an established trail every workout, go for an occasional bushwhack and break your own trail. Mix your speeds.

Nutritional Needs

Eat for energy. When it's cold, your metabolism is working over-time to maintain 98.6 degrees. Winter trails are no place for dieting. Clothing is only one defense against hypothermia. A key factor to maintaining your core body temperature is to feed the furnace. You need to burn calories to generate heat and, just like building a fire, you need to know which foods convert to energy quickly and which ones are for long-term sustenance. For a good fire you need kindling: sticks and logs. Complex carbohydrates like fruits burn quickly; simple carbohydrates like grains can be stored for the short term but burn easily; and fats burn slowest. All are important; all work to keep you warm and running like a finely tuned machine. If you are headed out for the day, have a hearty, guilt-free breakfast: pancakes, oatmeal, cereals, muffins with butter, eggs, sausage, bacon, bagels with cream cheese; this is the time to stoke up the fire. For the trail take along gorp, Granola bars, or energy bars to snack on throughout the day. If you're feeling the shivers, fruits or fruit juices will warm you the quickest. If you are on a long hike, carry a thermos of hot cider or hot orange juice; either will warm your core up quickly. Candy bars may taste great and be loaded with sugar, but they do not metabolize very fast.

Drink plenty of liquids. Among other contributors to hypothermia, dehydration is one of the leading causes. Liquids help digestion and the distribution of energy throughout your body. An adult should consume at least two liters per day. Don't wait until you are thirsty to drink; that's too late. Hydrate often. If you are headed out for a quick workout, have a tall glass of water before you go and take a bottle along. You can't over-hydrate.

Regardless of the intensity of your workouts, the overall benefits are well worth the time spent. It is a great way to stay in shape for running, hiking, and cycling when the snow finally melts in spring. Before going, however, check with your doctor to be sure you haven't any conditions that might be aggravated by snowshoeing.

Fun on the Trail

Exploring

Snowshoeing specifically for a workout is certainly beneficial, but, besides all the obvious health benefits, it is fun to just get in the fresh air. Hitting the trail with a friend for a day hike offers plenty of low-impact exercise without focusing on fitness. It's a little like having X-ray vision as you can see deeper into the forest as your favorite summer or fall trails radically change with the fallen leaves and blanket of snow.

When making plans, you will need to figure on traveling only half the distance you'd normally hike without the snow, even less if you are breaking trail. No matter how familiar you are with a hike, take along a map. With the change of pace and the fact that many of the landmarks you are used to will be buried, it's easy to get disoriented.

Knowing how to use a map and compass are basic outdoor skills. Even if you are just following trails, comprehension of maps, map legends, and how to orient a map to the real world is essential. At worst it could save you hours of bumbling around trying to get back to your car; at best it could save you from the dangers of spending a night in the snow or endangering others in an effort to rescue you. It can also provide a great deal of fun bushwhacking your own trails through the unknown. Don't rely on following your own tracks out of the woods, (remember Hansel and Gretel). Snow or wind can blow your tracks away or fill them in with drifting snow. It's best to observe the scenery in front and behind you as you travel and track your progress on a map. This makes it easier to backtrack.

Figure 16 **On the trail.**

Picnics

Public parks with permanent picnic tables and grills are made for winter cookouts. In summer, they are usually easily accessed by automobile; by winter the roads lay unplowed and inviting to skiers and snowshoeists.

Exhilarating fresh air invites good food. As mentioned before, food is important to staying warm, but there are other times when food can be a destination unto itself. A short or long hike with friends and family out to a secluded space tucked out of the wind in the pines, a ledge overlooking a snow-covered valley, or the side of a remote frozen waterfall is great fun. A picnic should be more than a handful of trail mix or a cold sandwich squashed in the bottom of your pack. It's a call to culinary creativity. It can be hot or cold and should involve many courses.

Prepare as much as you can ahead of time; it shortens the wait for food and allows for more social time. If you are serving crackers and cheese with pepperoni as an appetizer, or dip and veggies, do the slicing in the warmth of your kitchen, pack the food in resealable plastic bags, and serve immediately after the site is prepared. For messier items like marinades or sauces, double bag. Use lightweight, Lexan

Figure 17   **Off-trail snowshoeing to reach fresh powder.**

utensils and nonmetal cups that won't freeze to your lips or tongue when cold. A thermos of hot water provides the start to hot chocolate, tea, or instant soups.

Picnic Supplies: What to Pack

Pack a *small shovel* for clearing the table, cleaning out the grill, and cleaning up afterward.

Instead of dragging wood along or marring the forest by stripping the trees of dead branches, bring a small bag of *charcoal bricks* (to save weight carry only enough to use for cooking; it makes the trip out a lot lighter). Self-starting charcoal is easier to manage than hauling starter fluid along with you. Put the amount needed in a paper bag and then wrap it in a garbage bag to keep the starter solution from permeating your pack and food. (You can use the garbage bag later to carry out your trash.)

If there isn't a grill, bring your own *portable grill;* bring an *aluminum pie plate* for a charcoal bed and a *small folding grill.* It will make cleanup easier, especially if there are no grills where you have your cook-out.

If you bring along a few creature comforts, you may even forget it's winter. Cut up a closed-cell *foam sleeping pad* to sit or stand on; it will insulate you from the cold. Pack a highly compressible *parka* to pull on to stay warm during long breaks.

Load your supplies on a plastic sled.

Preparing a Site and Cleaning Up

When you arrive at your chosen site, pack down your space. This is a great group project and, with many feet, goes quite quickly. Once the snow is compressed, you can take your snowshoes off while you eat.

Don't build a wood fire without permission, and when you are done, spread the ashes over a wide area. This way you won't leave a pile of ugly black ashes and charred wood to be exposed when the snow melts.

Carry out whatever you have carried in.

Don't throw foiled products in the fire; they won't burn. Don't rely on Mother Nature to dispose of your trash. Take orange peels, banana peels, and apple cores home. The woodland inhabitants may not find a human diet kind to their digestive system or even to their liking.

Competition

People have been racing on snowshoes ever since the first person said, "Last person to camp is a rotten egg." Organized racing has a rich history of social-club competitions, especially in communities with a strong Franco/American heritage in the Northeast and Canada. Events are still often preceded by parades, with each team in colorful uniforms and carrying banners supported by drum and bugle corps. Races are held for all ages and sexes participating in sprints and walks ranging from 100 to 8,000 meters. Since the eighties, "citizen racing"

Figure 18

An impromptu snowshoe race.

has exploded. These races are open to both men and women, no matter the age. Runners have discovered the fun of trail running, and many cross-country ski centers have opened their trails and sponsored many events. Many manufacturers sponsor race series that match the 5K and 10K distances of summer running events—don't expect your times to be the same.

Snowshoeing attracts a number of unusual events, like springtime Pole, Paddle, and Paw races, which are triathlons of canoeing, cross-country skiing, and snowshoeing. Jerico, Vermont, hosts a Black Powder Biathlon, where participants dressed in historic costumes compete in a race that also includes marksmanship with muzzleloaders as part of the total score.

Snowshoeing is the easiest way to get out and enjoy winter; the only limits are your imagination. There are clubs to join and people to meet if you run out of ideas. Many winter resorts have opened trails and offer special snowshoe vacations.

Snowshoeing with Kids

Something magical happens when kids get on snowshoes. It could be that the experience is just so different and they have immediate success getting around, or it could be the sense of limitless freedom. Whatever the key, kids have an absolute blast. They seem to always have enough energy to explore around one more corner. If you can appeal to their curiosity and imagination, you always have enthusiastic hiking companions.

Successful trips come from making plans that the kids will enjoy. Kids are destination-oriented. Have a plan that they can understand, which makes it easy for them to troop along. Your future credibility depends on your plan, so be sure it is something the kids will enjoy or at least remember pleasantly. On longer hikes plan a variety of destinations. It is always easier to go farther if kids easily reach a milestone. It may be a bridge, an unusual old tree, or an interesting rock outcropping. The more you know about a trail, the more willing your short-legged followers are to being led.

Kids have a certain amount of obligatory resistance built into their genes. There is a fine line between encouraging them to go a little farther, staying out a little longer, and pushing them to a point where they will never want to go again. Let kids dictate the pace. You need to keep outings fun and interesting but be willing to call it a day when the fun factor has gone. Most kids won't be very excited about the idea of going for a walk. Certainly the novelty of wearing snowshoes makes it a little easier, but you still need to be sure the fun factor is high.

Start out with excursions that keep mileage as the lowest priority.

Figure 19 **Kids love snowshoeing.**

Activities

Appeal to their curiosity and imagination. Playing "Who lives in these woods?" is a great activity. Finding animal tracks and following them to their winter homes, figuring out what they had for dinner, and looking for animal highways in the woods are wonderful opportunities for discovery and easy ways to put time and distance out of the picture.

Bring along guidebooks that show animal tracks, birds, and even trees—they are great to feed kids' curiosity. Mice, squirrel, and rabbit tracks can still be adventures to follow. Assign points based on how common they might be. Learn how to identify the difference between dog and bear tracks. Depending on where you live, you might find deer, moose, or otter tracks.

Take time to make your own tracks. Deep, fresh snow invites making snow angels or building a snowman in the middle of nowhere. Draw pictures with snowshoe tracks.

Make up a scavenger hunt of things to find in the woods—tracks and trees, animal signs like seed piles, or rubbed bark.

Be sure to make time for some nonsnowshoeing fun. Play tag, take a sled to the local hill the "long way," or have a cookout with hot dogs and marshmallows on a stick.

Appropriate Dress

Dress your kids a little warmer than you would dress yourself, but don't overdress them. Be sure to surround them with a water-resistant shell and bring an extra pair of gloves or mittens. Kids love to be "in" the snow. Let them carry their own pack with their own trail "survival" gear: water, snacks, neck warmer, or stuffed animal. Fanny packs were made for kid adventures; they're small and easy to get on and off. Don't forget chapped-lip protection, sunscreen, and sunglasses; the elements are magnified with cold, dry winter air and the sun reflecting off the snow.

Most important, it is always better to quit while you are having fun and building only great memories. It always makes the next trip that much easier.

On the Trail:

Courtesy, Caution, and Easy Going

The winter world is a beautiful place, and there are so many ways to enjoy it. Here are a few things that will make your excursions more pleasant.

Trail Courtesy

Just because you can go pretty much anywhere with snowshoes doesn't mean you should. Make sure you have permission to use the trails you're on and you aren't trespassing. Who knows, while you are asking for permission, you may get a great tip of a magical place to visit.

If you are on a snowmobile trail remember two things: (1) You can hear snowmobiles, they can't hear you. When you hear a snowmobile coming, get off the trail in plenty of time to clear passage. (2) You are on *their* trails. Some club or other organization has worked hard to make those nice trails and bridges for snowmobiles, not pedestrians. Snowmobile riders have more right to be annoyed with your presence than you do with theirs.

If you go to a cross-country ski center, stay on the marked trails. As easy as it is for you to make your own new trail, it will add confusion to existing trail maps and create a liability nightmare for the operator. Plan frequent stops for water, snacks, and clothing adjustments. If you are uncomfortable, chances are others in your group are, as well.

Wherever you go, pack out your litter and leave only tracks.

Figure 20 **How *not* to cross over an obstruction. Stepping onto a rock or log with just the front of the snowshoe on the obstruction is an invitation to a fall.**

Caution

Bridging

One ticket to disaster, especially with wooden snowshoes, is bridging. Bridging is a situation in which you find the tip and tail of your snowshoe on a solid surface, and you, with all your weight, are suspended in the middle. The result can be an ugly break or a bend in shoes. Climbing over brooks, gullies, stonewalls, or blown-down trees

Figure 21

Crossing over an obstruction. Step up onto the rock or log with the lead foot, bring your other foot up, and then step down.

needs to be done deliberately. Climbing over trees or stonewalls requires a solid foot plant either on top of the obstacle or, if your legs are long enough, cleanly on the other side. A solid foot plant means your weight is centered on your foot. You'll need to have both feet on top of the obstacle before you step down, being careful to come down

with solid footing. If your inseam permits, sidestep over the obstacle, giving yourself enough room to place the next shoe. Again, be sure you have solid footing before you commit your weight (Figure 21). With gullies try to sidestep as close to the bottom as you can to make your straddle step as easy as possible.

Snowshoeing

Figure 22   **Checking out equipment before a day's trek.**

Figure 23 **A pleasant day of snowshoeing. But note the depressions around the trees in the background—potential traps.**

Traps

Scenic wanderings require some caution.

Fir trees: Fir trees that look so attractive with snow decorating their deep green bows can be dangerous traps. Consider the shape of most fir trees—a point at the top and wide at the base. Deep snow may be banked high up on the outside of the limbs, making a tree look deceptively short, when in actuality you may be many feet above the base. Because of the shape of the tree, snow collects on the outer branches and is not in a position to support weight underneath. If you get too close, you can actually fall into the tree and the limbs will prevent you from climbing back out.

Ice: Know where you are going. Covered by snow, a pond and a field can look the same. Just because ice supports snow doesn't mean it will support you. Open water and running water are good signs of caution. Scenic overviews may hide an unsupported cornice ready to break away. Resist the urge to peer over a wintry edge.

Snowshoeing

Trail Repairs

Nothing can ruin an outing faster than equipment failure. Usually it's something pesky—minor, not major—that will be the most annoying. A minimalist repair kit should fit easily into a zip-top bag and can be carried in a pocket or pack. The kit should include things that will provide a quick fix for broken bindings, torn decking, cracked frames, shoe repairs, and even blisters.

Here are some suggestions:

- ◆ *Electrical ties* can be used to hold broken laces or decks to the frames.

- ◆ *Duct tape* wrapped on a ski pole for easy access—what can't duct tape do?

- ◆ *Popsicle sticks* make easy splints for cracked frames.

- ◆ *Parachute cord* can be used for making a temporary binding.

- ◆ *All purpose pocket survival tool* or Swiss army knife.

What to Pack for the Trail

There are some essentials you should take along, even if you are going for just a half-day excursion.

Water: Stay hydrated. Hydration is crucial to maintaining your body temperature. Remember that you lose more moisture in winter than in summer.

First aid kit: Any time you go on a hike, regardless of the time of year, you should carry a small first aid kit. It should be simple and not more extensive than your medical knowledge. For most short day or half-day hikes, it should contain articles to prevent blisters, like moleskin, or to protect them, like Nuskin, if you get to "hot-spots" too late. Band Aids for cuts and scrapes are always a good idea. For good measure you can toss in adhesive tape and Popsicle sticks to splint broken or sprained digits. To be a real hero, bring along a few toe and hand warmer packets and a small roll of toilet paper.

Emergency food: Pack something you wouldn't eat unless you were really hungry; that way, it won't become a trail snack.

Map: Unless it's snowing, it should be pretty easy to follow your own tracks back to where you started. A map helps you know where you are going and shows you possible areas to be cautious. Look at it before you go. If you can't read a map, take a class.

Matches and fire starter: If you get stuck because of an injury or broken gear, or if you're lost, the heat is nice, but the smoke will help rescuers find you.

Space blanket: You can wrap a space blanket to hold in the heat or you can sit on it to prevent heat loss.

Easy Going

A couple of trail strategies will make your travels less work and more fun:

Zigzag Traversing

Climbing generates heat. The harder you work, the more heat you'll produce and the more you'll tax your energy reserves. The trick to controlling your heat on a climb is to limit the work.

The shortest distance to the top of a hill is a straight line up. But that's not necessarily the fastest way up, just the most work. Look for the easiest route of travel. Off trail you are empowered to choose grades that create a gradual ascent. By traversing you are in control of the work. It's the art of route selection. While going up, you should be able to carry on a conversation and enjoy the scenery.

Look at your destination and study the terrain that leads to it. Oftentimes you will see natural routes through the trees and along ridges over humps and hummocks, a sort of uphill slalom course. As you zigzag your way along, you are always gaining altitude. Sometimes you may travel only a few steps to gain the advantage; other times you may enjoy a long, gradual gain. Generally speaking, your pace will be faster while you exert less energy.

Share the Lead

Share the lead with trail companions when hiking in deep snow, and take turns breaking trail. Establish a rotation to lead, and don't let anyone break trail until they are tired. Depending on how tough the going is, you can rotate by time or, even easier, by steps—say twenty

Figure 24 **Gaiters.**

steps through the deep stuff and then fall to the back of the group and follow the packed trail. Heroics don't cut it in winter. If you get over-heated and sweaty, you put yourself and the rest of the group at risk of hypothermia.

Gear and Gadgets

Snowshoes and the right clothing will get you on the trail, but there are lots of little things that will make your time on the trail more enjoyable.

First and foremost, take along *ski poles*. These are so high on the list they might be considered essentials. Poles will help with balance, propulsion, and, in deep snow, they are used to recover from a spill. Adjustable, telescoping poles are the best. They're strong, the length can be adjusted to accommodate different snow conditions, and they can be compressed for travel. If you are running, longer cross-country ski poles will help you stride; if you are just walking, alpine poles will do. If you don't have big baskets on your poles, put some larger ones on; you'll appreciate the extra support in soft snow.

Take *gaiters* for over your boots. No matter how tightly you batten down the hatches, snow always has a way of working itself into your boots. A gaiter that covers your laces to your calf not only keeps your feet dry but also holds heat in your feet. Gore-Tex gaiters cost a little extra but are well worth the money because they let your feet breathe and stay even drier. If you've never worn gaiters, there is a little hook in the front that attaches to your laces and a strap that reaches under your arch to keep them from riding up.

A couple of versatile accessories to leave stuffed in your pack and pulled out on cold days for added warmth are a *fleece neck warmer* and a *balaclava*. The neck warmer is a little like a scarf but more manageable. Worn around the neck, it will cut the heat loss coming up through your outer layer and the gap between your collar and hat. It can be pulled up to protect your chin and even higher to serve as a face mask. The fleece is soft and it dries quickly. A balaclava is a great addition on really blustery days. Worn under a hat, it will protect the back of your neck and cover your chin and nose to protect them from frostbite.

Pack along *sunglasses* or *goggles*. They're not just for sun protection; driving wind and blowing snow can put you into a permanent squint. And don't forget *lip balm, sunscreen,* and *moisturizing lotion* to protect your skin from the harsh winter air.

Appendix

Snowshoe Sources

Alchemy Snowshoes
12554 Kirkham Court
Poway, CA 92064
(877) 748-4808
or (619) 486-8940
www.alchemysnowshoes.com

Baldas Snowshoes
Baldas USA, Inc.
1101 Wetherburn Court
Winston-Salem, NC 27104
(336) 659-9990
  Popular European snowshoes
now available in the USA.

Classic Snowshoes
www.classicsnowshoes.com
  A Web-based company offering
old snowshoes for collectors and
decorators.

Faber Snowshoes
Caribou Cry Ltd.
2215a Dundas Street East
Toronto, Ontario L4X 2X2
Canada
(888) 553-2553
or (905) 602-0917
www.cariboucry.com

Gastrem (1993) Inc.
1100 Dr. Penfield, Suite 118
Montreal, Quebec H3A 1A8
Canada
(514) 847-0212
www.gastrem-snowshoes.com

Traditional snowshoes made at
the Huron Village Indian
Reservation near Quebec City.

Havlick Snowshoe Company
2513 State Highway 30,
Drawer QQ
Mayfield, NY 12117
(800) 867-7463
or (518) 661-4644
www.havlicksnowshoe.com
  Aluminum-frame and wood-
frame snowshoes.

Little Bear Snowshoes
Spring Brook Manufacturing
2591 B 3/4 Road
Grand Junction, CO 81503
(800) 655-8984
or (970) 241-8546
www.littlebearsnowshoes.com
  Snowshoes "for the whole
family," with many specialty
snowshoes for kids.

MSR
P.O. Box 24547
Seattle, WA 98124
(800) 877-9677
or (206) 624-7048
www.msrcorp.com

Northern Lites
1300 Cleveland
Wausau, WI 54401
(800) 360-LITE
www.northernlites.com
  Lightweight, aluminum-frame
snowshoes.

Prater Snowshoes
3740 Cove Road
Ellensburg, WA 98926
(509) 925-1212
www.adsnet.net/prater

Redfeather Design, Inc.
4705-A Oakland Street
Denver, CO 80239
(800) 525-0081
www.redfeather.com
Fine showshoes in a wide range of designs. Great Web site with events calendar and racing information.

Sherpa Snowshoe Company
9640 South 60th Street
Franklin, WI 53132
www.sherpasnowshoes.com

TiptoeSnowshoes.com
5068 SW Technology Loop #117
Corvallis, OR 97333
(541) 758-2049
www.tiptoesnowshoes.com

Tubbs Snowshoe Company
52 River Road
Stowe, VT 05672
(800) 882-2748
or (802) 253-7398
www.tubbssnowshoes.com
The world's largest snowshoe manufacturer. Wide choice of models to suit anyone. Informative Web site.

Wilcox and Williams
6001 Lyndale Avenue South, Suite A
Minneapolis, MN 55419
(800) 216-0710

www.protocom.com/protomall/wandw
Kits to make your own traditional snowshoes.

Wing Enterprises, Inc.
1325 West Industrial Circle
Springville, UT 84663-3100
(877) SNOWSHOE
www.powderwings.com
Manufacturer of "compactible" Powder Wings snowshoes, designed to break down into a fanny pack and reassemble without tools.

Yowie Snowshoes Pty. Ltd.
122 Kororoit Creek Road
Williamstown, Victoria 3016
Australia
+61-3-9397-2115 (international)
or 03-9397-2115 (in Australia)
www.yowies.com.au
Lightweight, flexible snowshoes with no moving parts.

Yubashoes
PRIDE Sacramento
555 Display Way
Sacramento, CA
(800) 550-6005
or (916) 783-5266
Manufacturers of fine Yuba snowshoes. Yubashoes is a branch of PRIDE, a nonprofit dedicated to employing physically challenged workers.

Yukon Charlie's Snowshoes
P.O. Box 160
Buzzards Bay, MA 02532
(508) 759-0061
www.yukoncharlie.com

Index

TRAIL MIX

BASIC★ESSENTIALS™
CROSS-COUNTRY SKIING

JOHN MOYNIER
SECOND EDITION

Whatever trails you choose to follow, whether on skis, snowshoes, or snowboard, **The Globe Pequot Press** can provide you with the information you need to enjoy winter to the fullest.

Learn the basics of mastering your sport as well as the specifics of *regional* winter sport destinations and accommodations.

Ramble down hiking paths, cruise through open fields, and visit ski-touring facilities with these books as your trail guides to fun and adventure.

MID-ATLANTIC winter sports GUIDE
by John Phillips

The Complete Guide to Downhill Skiing, Snowboarding, Cross-country Skiing, Snow Tubing, and More Throughout the Mid-Atlantic Region

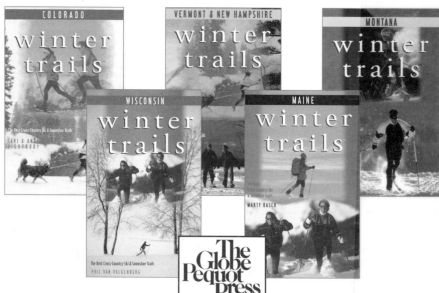

COLORADO
winter trails

VERMONT & NEW HAMPSHIRE
winter trails

MONTANA
winter trails

WISCONSIN
winter trails

MAINE
winter trails

The Globe Pequot Press